"I sense you in all of me"

Honeysuckle Me

by Carla M. Cherry

THE SECOND EDITION

iiPUBLISHING

Honeysuckle Me
Copyright © 2021 by Carla M. Cherry

Second Edition

Copyright notice
All rights reserved. No part of this book may be reproduced in any form or by any electronic or mechanical means, including information storage and retrieval systems, without permission in writing from the author or publisher, except for the use of brief quotations in a book review.

Cover design by tonii

ISBN: 978-1-7362167-8-1

Printed in the United States of America

iiPUBLISHING
New York, NY
www.toniiinc.com

Note

Honeysuckle Me is my third book of poetry, and it was comprised of poems written in 2017. I self-published the first edition of *Thirty Dollars and a Bowl of Soup* through Wasteland Press in the same year. I am extremely grateful to the beautiful work that Tim Veeley, president of Wasteland Press, did on the formatting and designing cover art for my first edition, and I will always be proud of it.

Thanks to iiPublishing, I have been able to transition from self-publishing to traditional publication. This new edition of Honeysuckle Me from iiPublishing includes four new poems.

Acknowledgements

As always, much love to my mother, Paula Cherry, my son Khari, my niece Anike, and the rest of my family and friends. I am deeply indebted to my lifelong friend, Dr. Tanya Manning-Yarde, for her encouragement and poetic insight, to Peter-Charles Seaton for his mentorship, honesty, and rigor, and to Abiodun Oyewole for his friendship, discerning eye, and listening ear.

CONTENTS

Written By Herself	2
Pyrophobia	6
Bobbing	8
Diastema	13
Pith	14
Flourish	16
Double Dutch	20
The Way	22
Last Dance	24
Chances	26
Every Tub Must Stand on Its Own Bottom	28
Epitome	29
Explorers	30
If I Were Finished	32
For Love of the Word	34
Proem	36
A Little Magic	37
Descant	38
Guilt	41
Midnight Mischief	42
Yoni	43
Sensibility	44
Tattoo	45
Under the New Moon	47
As A Womanist/Feminist	48
Sister to Sister	50
Whet	55
For the Lovers	56
Blood and Soil	58
Love, by the Numbers	68
Scattered Legacy	70
Afterword & The Author	75

"Honey, suckle me…"

Written by Herself
After "Written by Himself" by Gregory Pardlo

I was born after hours, Albert Einstein Hospital.
My mother frozen by epidural needle
Peggy and Boston, John and Lena
Milton and Florence whispering my name
my father convinced it was his idea to name me Carla.
Carla Thomas sang a favorite song, Gee Whiz.
I was born to patchwork quilts and afghans
between the Bronx and Hudson Rivers
Fulton Terrace across the street from I.S. 148
where street hoods pulled a knife on my father
the night he volunteered to guard the school.
I was shrouded by a white satin dress and blessed.
Passed around to hands that kneaded dough
poured hot water into salt and peppered corn meal
pressed into patties
fried in a cast iron skillet
threaded a bobbin
pressed foot to pedal
sewed me dresses for Easter Sunday
shined my patent leather shoes.
I was given to oak trunk arms and nestling laps,

folk bent at the waist asking for some sugar.
Salty sticky pecks pleased them.
They taught me many things,
like the two strikes I was born with were not my fault
but I had better work for what I needed and wanted.
My pockets filled with bubble gum
Now-a-laters
Jolly rancher wrappers
hairpins that had been poking my scalp while I played tag.
I was born with a little jaundice.
Encouraged superstitious.
Don't step on sidewalk cracks.
Near-sightedness an expected burden.
I gave birth.
His middle name, Ngozi, means blessing.
Suspicious of fate, I made plans, budgets, grocery lists
to-do lists, dream and safety graduate schools.
I was born whole, through my mother's hole,
my great-great grandparents' freedom dreams come full circle.
My Uncles Robert, Ralph, James Reginald,
and my mother, born underneath hot towels to steam them out,
were Black babies banned from Kentucky hospitals.
I played beneath honey locust trees.
Stomped through sandboxes.
Swung around tire swings that sometimes made me throw up.

Sometimes the air blew grit in my eyes.
When hurricane winds rattled our windows before my father
drew a giant X across them with masking tape and
told us not to worry when we cried.
Donny Hathaway drifted up and down the stairs
while my father made pancakes.

Read all the books my head could hold.
Distressed by facts and figures
until Daddy taught me to count my change faster than the cash registers.

Wily entanglement of Africa, Europe, and the Cherokee nations,
I was born blood-on-a-white-shirt stubborn.
Jumped in a pool without looking when I was 4,
My father diving after me.

Ain't I a woman?
Yes I am.
Always wanted a brother.
Had a cute cool crazy funny sister that I wish would haunt me
once in a while.

I was born mystified.
Transmogrified in the eyes of some
properly dignified by the mirror attached to my bureau
laughed through the hall of mirrors every time, and
this horror story that is America.
I am making my own happy ending.
I was born, approved, via exordium of Milton and Florence of Kentucky,
Peggy, Boston, John and Lena,
who toiled North Carolina cotton fields
trees too far away to give them shade
gnats and mosquitoes and white folks taking what they wanted.
The Color Line was the greatest problem of the twentieth century.
What kind of eraser will we need?
I read The Emperor's New Clothes before I could read
about a baby set in a basket on water.
Armed with parables about fishes and loaves,
I never walk alone.

Pyrophobia: there is a reason why

I was four when the burning began.
As Grandmother had done to her, Mother
had me perched on our yellow step stool right next to the stove,
open jar of blue Ultra Sheen on the countertop.

Plastic comb for sectioning, hot comb on the burner, warming.
Paper towel atop a cotton one, for the embers.
Towel draped around shoulders like devil's ivy.
Every few moments, she lifted the hot comb from the flame,
blew wisps of air on it.

And like an osprey diving towards a trout,
she swooped down into my puffy kinks,
searing my hair straight, one tuft at a time,
bergamot oil and petroleum jelly wafting through the house.

Sometimes she burned the helix of my ears; made me jump.
Hold still! she snapped. One day, thinking of them, I blew out the flame.
Imagining explosion, dead husband and daughters,
Mother had nails in her voice: *Don't ever do that again.*

As a mature woman, I steal snuggles in Mother's lap.
She strokes my kinky coils;

I comb her textured, silver silky hair. Still,
fearing fiery burn on fingers, I won't light a match.

I never light candles for any birthday cake;
have already blown a thousand dandelion wishes
and faith outpaces my need for luck.

Don't need to light a pilot light to cook.
I don't throw big parties; don't bring me cans of Sterno.
A dinner for two? Yes. Candlelit? No.

Flick off just one light switch.
There will be enough darkness
prodding passions, and ample, butter soft light
to peer into our souls.

Bobbing

Was hard to witness
Mommy's day to day
underwire ritual.

That center gore never quite sat right.
She closed her bra
on the tightest setting to raise the cups.

Straps planted riverbed grooves into
the girdle of my mother's shoulders.

I watched her on her wash days
bend over the tub on her knees.
Streams of black swirl
rushed towards the drain
as she beat back the encroach of silver
with black dye.

Housed her hips inside creased slacks.
Shrouded pretty legs
within knee-length skirts.

Stuffed her wide feet
into narrow high heels.
They squeezed her baby toes.
After 22 years of retirement
the natural color of her nails
hasn't returned.

She swayed to and from
her desk,
bosses' offices,
and the coffee machine.
Took dictation in shorthand.
Read first drafts of their handwritten letters.
Corrected poor spelling and grammar.
Produced correspondence at 150 words per minute.

When I visited her at work
my neck burned hell-hot
when those Misters called
her Paula, not Mrs. Cherry.
She's a married woman,
I thought.

I smiled politely through the introductions
Because I knew how
our household needed her income too.

When I read that bras
constrict lymphatic flow,
I undid the hook and eye.

Lettum fly outta the frame of those cups.

Land like a needle on vinyl
when a DJ drops a beat.

I know it ain't supposed to be
the kinda thang to
broadcast to mixed company,
but in my boyfriend's palm,
his generous lips
nudging netherly tickle,
they're firmer than ever.

Now that my breasts
have been riding
pandemic pretty
I will hate having to
tuck them back into that apex--
but I can't have the outline of my nipples
visible against silk or cashmere.

If I had canvas
and talent,
I'd paint
Mommy and me,
twirling bands of our bras with our hands
skipping towards the horizon
our bosoms in holy dance.

Diastema

Brushed my teeth
to a low beam gleam. Smiled

in the mirror and thought about
the gap between my top front teeth that closed

on its own by the time I was 13.
Was feeling myself until I thought about

my mother's shy smile
as she told me about going to the Bahamas

and the men who thought her
a sexy beauty because of hers.

She is 80, looks 60,
always has money.

I can only pray
for her kind of luck.

Pith

My mechanic offers me a seat in his office.
I inhale broadly.
The sting of motor oil.
Like my father after he finished fixing somebody's car.
A flash of me watching him at the sink washing his hands,
scrubbing the gunk underneath his nails with a tiny brush.

An elder walks in, and sits six feet away.
I am so thankful, she says.
Today is my birthday. I'm 70.
I can tell from the upward swing of her cheekbones
above her blue paper mask,
the crinkle of her eyes, that she is smiling.
Happy Birthday, I say.
She flexes her legs and electric blue toenails.
That's a blessing.
She's retired after 40 years in human services.
My husband is good, she says, but I always had my own money.
I laugh. *Yes, my mother always told me to do that.*
We talk about why we still live in New York.
For me, it is family, work, and culture.
For her, her daughters, and grandchildren. Her son.
He is about to turn 49. Like me, I say.
I got a few years left, God willing, she says.
He's been in and out of jail.
He's been homeless for a year.
I'm so sorry.
He needs to get his life together. I keep telling him.
I don't want to hear all that, he says.
He can't stay in my house.
I'm not going to let him kill me.

Does he have any children of his own?
No, she jumps out of her chair and stomps her feet.
Praise God, he doesn't.
He can't care for himself or his sisters. He asks them for help.
It's hard when you do everything right to raise them and they go a different way.
He argues with me, but he doesn't lay a hand on me.
I brought him in this world, and I'll take him out.
I laugh. *My mother used to say that too.*

When her car is ready, she smiles as she walks out of the door.
We wish each other God's good will.

One might accuse her of oversharing.
That because we were in a room together
she was triggered by a sense of false intimacy.
That because we are both black women
she had a similarity bias and I should have nodded politely
or changed the subject away from what my mother calls dirty laundry.
But I know what it is to need a new ear to listen.
To feel like gravity is not enough to ground us.
I give thanks my son has never been arrested,
pray this woman's son finds his way,
and that she is around to see it.
She is the type of older woman Daddy advised me
to add to my circle of friends,
the kind who knows how to sucker-punch Sorrow and
paint her nails the color of the ocean.

Flourish

Sometimes while I am walking down my block
I hear somebody say,
Damn
What is that smell?

Sometimes somebody stepped on
ginkgo biloba seeds--
orange,
round like cherries,
smell like rotten peaches.

Ginkgo biloba
grows full in Northern sun
inhales pollution, exhales fresh air.
Unbothered by winter's rock salt.

Leaves like fans.
If you're born here, you rep for your city.
Where I'm from, we cross our arms for the BX.

We love our fireworks in July,
but baby,
they got nothing on the arboreal explosion
of yellow every autumn.

The ginkgo biloba thrives in tight spaces
resists disease
and when it comes to soil type
it isn't fussy.

It's just like those of us who grew up in
shoulder to shoulder apartment buildings
shared walls thrumming with congas and R&B bass
who ride racing iron horses over
spit-out sunflower seeds,
coffee cups stashed under the seats,
copies of AM New York left on top
coughing and sneezing outside the elbow,
5 million pairs of hands on poles,
cigarette stank breath and smoky clothing
wide hips and/or man-spreading legs tight against yours
cuz God knows we're all tired and need a seat.
An open book or your phone are the best targets for your eyes,
and if you're still on after 10 p.m.
you'd better move if you see somebody stumbling
and bent over at the waist.

Urban planners recommend the male ginkgo bilobas
to avoid the slime of stepped on female seeds.

But where I live in the Bronx
our concrete and streets ain't just for sneakers, man-sweaty basketballs.
High heels, open-toed sandals, jellies,
they got you.
Buildings stand up
to the bounce of Big Ma,
Abuela
aunties
calling us to come back upstairs
clothing racks on Fordham Road crammed
with dresses and leggings
built to hug the brown and black body positive.

Why should we experience beauty and life without
the mess that comes with being female?

I once bled onto the seat of a taxicab
when my fibroids were at their worst
and my pad had overflowed
but
you should meet my son
a 6-foot vessel of
golden brown skin,
light,
compassion,
poetry.
He is my sun,
my shade
when I am joyful,
and my shelter on the sad days.

Double Dutch

Didn't have a jump rope for our field trip.
One of my girls suggested telephone wire.
Ran to the corner store, got a black one.

Went to the park.
In groups of three, we took turns, and
>	I was back on my Bronx courtyard,
>	rocking back and forth
>	to the beat of our white canvas rope hitting concrete
>	before jumping in,
>	praying the ropes wouldn't hit me in the face,
>	knock off my glasses.

>	I was one of those lateral jumpers--side to side.

>	Like Daddy used to say--as he veered away from crowded highways--
>	always have more than one way to get to your destination.

>	Never was quick enough to skip,
>	clap my hands,
>	tap on my knees or ankles,
>	hop over those ropes with just one foot.

>	Was just trying to get to one up, two up
>	turn around once or twice
>	hop up in the air
>	land
>	resume the jumping.

Never seemed to get past three up
before I stepped on one of the ropes
and had to wait before I could jump back in
or be one of the turners;

had to count aloud
to keep my arms swinging the ropes on beat.
To be double-handed was sin.

With my girls, now,
I turned the rope in perfect time,
Huffing and puffing, but
kept perfect count:
One up 2 3 4 5 6 7 8 9
Two up 2 3 4 5 6 7 8 9
and
when it was my turn to jump

I dove in,
hopped back and forth to the beat,
held my shirt down like we used to
so our breasts wouldn't bounce,

hoping my girls saw me as
an older version of them,
and would fight our reading and writing together
a little less come Monday.

The Way

Men, step up to the women.
Offer up your hand,
Smile, say your name,
Ask if they'd like to dance.

Offer her your arm.
Lead her to the floor.
Count to three on beat.
Dip her on four.

It can be hard to follow.
But ladies, take heed.
Let it all go.
Let the men lead.

Skirts and dresses flowing
No one in their seats.
Black people showing love
to an eight-count beat.

Do your basic
to an eight-count beat
do the fake
to an eight-count beat
cross over
to an eight-count beat
half right
to an eight-count beat
half left
to an eight-count beat.
Take a stroll
to an eight-count beat
extended right
to an eight-count beat
stroll and skip

to an eight-count beat
double left
to an eight-count beat
box right
to an eight-count beat
backpedal
to an eight-count beat
kickstand
to an eight-count beat
tic man
to an eight-count beat
Suzy q
to an eight-count beat
sexy walk
to an eight-count beat
pity pat now,
to an eight-count beat
shuffle
to an eight-count beat
parade walk
to an eight-count beat
ballroom right
to an eight-count beat
spin and return
to an eight-count beat
roll back
to an eight-count beat
butterfly
to an eight-count beat
side step
to an eight-count beat

And when the song fades out,
hug them for the chance,
to express black love,
through an eight-count dance.

Last Dance

She floated into the bar with the October breeze.
Hung up her jacket on a hook.
Eased into the bathroom, smoothed her black dress.
Checked the glossiness of her maroon lipstick,
that the scarlet polish on every nail was unchipped,
every strand of hair twisted into uniform submission,
every eyelash evenly coated black, waterproof,
and arched like her back on long-ago nights.

Greeted this one/that one,
hugs and light smacks of lips on cheeks.
Sashayed to the darkened back.
Squinted against the flashing disco lights.
Surveyed the crowded floor.
Baby powder to facilitate spins in every corner,
its scent overpowered by fried chicken wings and perspiration.
Partner after partner for four hours.
 sips of water in between until the last song.

At last he approached with a smile and outward gesture.
She arose slowly; let him lead her to the center.
He pulled her into him.
She tapped out the beat against his right shoulder blade.
He dipped her. Deeply.

She giggled, knew he was strong enough.
For five minutes, it was hard chest brushing against soft one.
Two sets of manicured hands: holding, releasing.
Quick drags of fingertips against palms.
His eyes, her eyes averted from the curve of her, his bottom lip.
Her waist, her heat, charming his hands towards the arc of her derriere.
He spun her instead, too many times to count,
and she stepped back on her eight, just right, each time.
His hands, her waist, her shoulders.
Their has-beens, why-nots, what ifs, drowned out by bumping bass.
The chorus faded out, and then it was over.
Her smile, his smile. Brief, tight embrace.
Waves and hugs all around.

When she got to her car,
she clutched her scarf, untied its knot.
Traced the patches of cobalt blue,
the same color as the shirt that he wore as promised,
so she would know
he missed her just as much.
She held it to her face.
Inhaled Egyptian musk.

Chances

Saw all the pics and realized--
        forgot about the solar eclipse.

Had been in bed, blinds closed,
        watching TV, alone, kind of liking it.

Hadn't remembered to buy those special sunglasses.
        Would never risk retinal burn for something available online.

Thought it pointless to be excited about the two minutes it took for
        the moon to align with the sun to block its light.

Beautiful fleeting things: comets, shooting stars, passionate love,
        turn me indigo blue

but so did the pics of arcs of light,
        people smiling.

Looked it up, discovered:
        Great-great-great Cherokee Grandmother

might have led us outside to stop
        that giant frog in the sky

from eating the sun with drumming and
        whistling and yelling to the heavens.

Longing for what was
        is superior to longing for what could have been;

should have been out there
        dancing in sunny shadows.

A picture of the ocean, a poem about a kiss,
        are inferior to waves crashing against my legs,
        a man's lips meandering mine.

Got a calendar and healthy heart.
        There is space to make myself present,
        avoid missing more beautiful fleeting things.

Every Tub Must Stand on Its Own Bottom

Grandma,
if you're still watching over me
I hope you have seen

I have done
as you did

when your marriage,
romances
grew cold like an Arctic wind--
        hung up
          erased numbers
          threw away the baubles
          of those Trillium type of lovers.

If you're listening when I pray,
could you tug God's sleeve a little?

I know that we come in,
go out of,
this world alone
but it sure is nice
if there's someone there
holding your hand
begging you to stay
when you're beckoned
to the light.

Epitome

My doctor said
I should lift
weights
to build
my strength
but
I heard that
butterflies
in the Amazon
sit on the faces
of crocodiles/
drink
their tears
to
glean the salt.
Man,
I want to learn
how to be
as bad-ass
as that.

Explorers

Use it or lose it
ain't enough
to scare me
into soul-sullying
aura swapping
with nomadic lovers.

I, watermelon juicy,
am waiting on
the man who wants to
share every sunrise,
cups of blue lotus tea
with honey, who would

drive us upstate
somewhere we could
rent a canoe.

With earth brown hands
wrapped around his paddles
he could lead our vessel
in a straight line downriver,

licks, laps of water
against the sides and underbelly
our only music
as we forge ahead
until afternoon's peak
and the sighting
of a small dock,
somewhere.

We could port.
Lay down
on opposite sides.
Linger, legs dangling.
Feet, water dipped.

The rattle and buzz
of the cicada courtship song
our concert in crescendo, diminuendo,
fingertips rising, falling between
thenar spaces,
interdigital folds.

If I Were Finished

Wouldn't my napkin be in my plate?

Please don't hover.
Yes,
I will order dessert.
In time.

What is the rush?

It's not that crowded in here.

I like to savor
each flavor,
each moment,
the curve of his lashes,
as I size him up from across the table.

Feeling this brother right now.

    He looks in my eyes as we talk.

    Asked me about favorite lessons I've taught.
    He's read every book Toni Morrison wrote.
    Loves every song Prince ever sung.
    Challenged me to a game of Scrabble for our next date,
    and wants to go dancing the date after that.

I'll take a scoop of chocolate ice cream
(non-dairy, if you please)
to cool my red-hot tongue,
and
this sudden desire to rush into sweetness.

For Love of the Word

I read at open mics--get some snaps, a couple of "I like thats", some
Hmmmms.
Would love to be one of those poets provoking
foot stomping and spontaneous cries.

Talent ain't a thing to be purloined, so I
accepted an invitation to meet modern-day Great Poet.
He offered me a seat, savory salmon cakes, and fried green tomatoes.

Read two of my poems aloud for him.
Sounds like you're reading a grocery list, he scolded.
Eggs. Cheese. Bread.

He re-read my poems for me, caressing each phoneme with his baritone.
Don't be a poet that can write but not perform!
Scoffed at the lifeless Langston Hughes album he once bought:
He blew my high.

With Lover,
I am like a toddler now.
He is teaching me how to speak,

to wedge pencil between teeth,
press tongue on roof of my mouth, manipulate
masseter, temporalis, medial and lateral pterygoids
so I can project my voice.

There is pleasure in the short and quick
but slower, longer, deeper is always better, so
I am learning to breathe from my diaphragm.

To pace. To focus my eyes on one word at a time, to each its own timbre.
Tone. Pitch. Poems as songs on sheet music.
Vary between treble and bass clefs.

I am learning to trust, to let go, to let in.
My head, held between his hands,
hair lathered with peppermint shampoo;
in between his knees,
my scalp soothed with lemongrass oil
through poetic recitations.

Fall asleep to the pulse of his heart.
Spoon tight enough for our pores to kiss.

He feels me in his bones.
I am learning to love again.

Proem

Ever since I've been in your arms

      I am a ray of sunlight
      the color green
      fallen lilac blossoms
      tiptoes on the wing of a butterfly
      the whirr of a hummingbird's wings
      the roots of a baobab tree
      mirror image of moonlight on water
      lyrics to a ballad sung in contralto
      first dip in a warm bubble bath
      a spritz of perfume
      honey on lips
      a chocolate covered anything
      cascading drops of jojoba oil down spine
      the tickle of a whisper
      the bite of an earlobe
      coils of kinks around fingers
      the crest and crash of waves
      sage words on a page.

A Little Magic

He cupped my chin with his right hand,
gazed into my eyes when he said, "I love you".
His pupils, dilated.
I'd read somewhere that was a sign of truth, but still
that night, while he slept, I was rambling around my garden,
flashlight in hand, until I found my patch of periwinkle.
Pulled some up.
After my first love broke up with me, Auntie told me--
Always grow you some periwinkle, girl.
See the way the vines cling?
Took them back in the house. Sat at my sewing table.
Intertwined blossoms, vines, even lengths of yellow and blue ribbons.
Fashioned two festoons.
Put mine around my neck. Crept back into bed.
Watched him sleep.
Soon as he cracked open his eyes, I said,
Wear this. Please.
He winced. Lifted himself erect.
Cupped my chin.
"I said I love you. And I'm here to stay."
Pupils dilated.
He pulled me into his chest.
I hiccupped and my stomach rumbled.
He laughed.
Blew cool air down my back.
I love you too.
I eased my flowery yoke off my neck.
Crumbled them both.
Tossed them on the floor.

Descant

If you have the right equipment
for the right borehole
you can hear what the earth sounds like--
a rumble of thunder.

Who is he, this man
humming
growling
gnawing
osculating
lips and nipples
steeping tongue in every curve/crevice
turning me misty/spurting/gushy.
This man, brought to his knees,
gorging my waters like I am
Nalubaale
Tanganyika
Malawi
Turkana
Kivu

Rukwa
Mweru
Rutanzige,
like he was dying of thirst before he met me.

This man who shaved shroud--
        decades of black wisps cascading to the floor.
Stooped to look at me, unveiled.
Snapped a photo that captured every slope, every layer.
Called me beautiful.

Is this man the one, this unraveling mystery,
        whose tongue is trowel to my cerebrum
        and repository of my life story, hopes, dreams
        who fingers my navel
        whose moans bounce off my walls
        whose plowing/determined furrowing towards my fornix
        tickles/tingles me trembling.

When he hits that bottommost point,
will he hear the rumble of thunder.

Guilt

Sorry it took so long
for me to clock in
but my hair was
all tangled around his fingers
and we had to
watch the sunrise.

Midnight Mischief

In my past life, I must have been one of those women
who got banished from the village, burned at the stake,
for dancing down the primrose path.

Who gets hot looking at an empty bottle of lotion?
Queen Helene's. It leaves me dry,
makes me long for you.

Come over.
Let me trace your tattoos with my tongue.
Honey, suckle me. Let me fill my mouth with you.

Let your fingers do that red light in the basement,
last song, slow drag
down my spine, backs of thighs, knees, calves.

Enter, exit, enter, exit at every angle as I rock your hips.
Entangle your hands in my hair.
Whisper/wail my name. Wake the neighbors if you want.

But this time, when you explode, let it be all over me.
Be my Lotion.
Massage your milk over every crook and contour.

You make my skin water soft.
Ever put your hand on top of a body of water?
It bounces against your palm, glides across your fingers, like my skin.

Yoni

The bass in his moans is
the backbeat to our love song.

Awed by its beauty, I asked him:
*What does it feel like
when our love muscles are mingling?*

He said,
*If you really want an inkling of your yoni magic
bake an apple pie.*

*After it cools a little
penetrate the crust with your index finger
until it reaches the bottom of the pan. Wiggle it.*

Hadn't done that since I was
a naughty giggling girl
standing on momma's yellow step stool
rummaging through her glass bottles of spices
to sniff out what, on occasion,
made the kitchen smell
like
like
apples
hot sugar
cloves
nutmeg
cinnamon.

Sensibility

Cinnamon--the ass-kicking super spice!

anti-viral
anti-fungal
anti-cancer
conquering cholesterol
minifying blood sugar.

Worth more than gold
in the days of ancient Kemet,
if you got it, and you'd just use a dash.

With 12-inch-tall containers stacked in the spice aisle
I refuse to use
my teaspoon to measure
sprinkles of cinnamon in my
tea
oatmeal
banana pudding.

Cinnamon.
It is to memory as what chocolate is to womanly wetness.

Sometimes, when he is irking me,
my ways are chafing him,
I get it down from the shelf,
lift the lid and inhale,

conjure our nuzzles by the fire
my feet in the warmth of his hand.

Honey,
I'd baptize him
in cinnamon,
if he'd let me.

Tattoo

He got the likeness of a woman
emblazoned on his left shoulder
a year after he began cuddling me
nights,
Saturday mornings,
like the cocoa butter lotion I wear
is adhesive,
sticking to me until I sweat.
When we kept the lights on
she hovered over my face
fully buxom
narrow-waisted
belly flat as a CD.
I would wonder why
she couldn't have curves that spill
over denim jeans
since he's always
burying his finger in my navel
slapping my backside
lifting my breasts
to watch them bounce
sighing about the way they ride.
Last night he caught me staring at her
after he got out of the shower.
He smiled.
"It's Nefertiti. I got it because they always only show her head."
He reached into his backpack and brought out
what he had been working on for several nights while I slept.
"I made these to celebrate the mother and lover in you."
He eased a black lava bracelet around my right wrist.
Clasped a black lava necklace around my neck.
Got down on one knee and wrapped
a string of tiny glass yellow
and blue beads around my waist.
"There's all kinds of beautiful."
I gave his left shoulder a lingering kiss.

Under the New Moon

Before shedding my clothes on the floor,
I turned off the light.
I like it dark, I said. Retreated undercover.
That's crazy, he said, and got up.
Opened the blinds.
A flood of pearly light.
He extended his hand. I took it, and he gently pulled me out of bed.
Walked me to the window.
We stood there, awash in white silvery aura.
He held my hands.
Look at me, he said.
My eyes met his.
We stood there, in silence.
He let go of my hands.
Traced the outline of collarbone.
Twin mounds of me.
My outer banks.
Ridges.
Two other twin mounds of me.
Silvery light reflected off his widening mouth.
I reached around him for the lamp.
Turned on the lights.
Struck by mal du pays
for his Buffalo Woman,
his mouth watered.
Twin mounds of me.
Gave him no time to close the blinds.

As A Womanist/Feminist

I can
>wonder aloud why Woman is missing from the Holy Trinity,
>demand with my vote, voice, and dollars
>that we unravel sociopolitical supports of patriarchy

and find it easy to love a man
who led me to my cabinet, said,
Now I am only going to show you this once,
pulled down all the spices
whose names I won't repeat here, or
elsewhere,
for a rub that goes three generations back.

Next time he comes over, he is going to bake
a sweet potato pie.
I'm stepping out of the kitchen for that one--
some mysteries don't need deciphering.

He rolls up his sleeves to
>wash my dishes until they squeak and sparkle,
>take out the garbage so I can cook cleanly
>and in aromatic peace,
>check my oil and my tire pressure.

When we walk to his car
before he takes my hand in his
he steps around me so that he is adjacent to the street.

Told me--
As long as I'm around, you'll always have a ride to work.

When I get home, and I want it,
my feet are in his hands, and he is
naming the parts of the body his fingers are kneading/healing--
Brain. Eyes. Ears. Heart. Lungs. Kidney. Pancreas. Spleen.

When I cook, I fix his plate first.

When he aches, I straddle him,
sweet almond oil in my palms, for
circumgyrations across the geography
of his neck/shoulder blades/spine.

And he always awakens to something sweet--
        a bunch of grapes,
        a spoonful of grapefruit,
        a slice of pineapple,
        my minty or tangy lips.

Sister to Sister
for Leslie Jones

Girl, being six feet tall,
with a big mouth,
looking like you can fight,
of a certain age,
and single, ain't easy.

I know why you lied on Conan about seeing someone.
Hard feeling like you have terrible luck with men, that they don't like you.

Not every man has the courage to jump at the sun.

Used to think you'd have more luck staying close to the ground:
toning it down,
not swiveling your neck and
bugging your eyes,
breathing from your diaphragm,
standing up straight,
speaking in softer tones,
smiling until each dimple deepens in each cheek,
adopting a breezy kind of walk for your six-foot frame.
Give men time to contemplate your earthy skin, full lips, full everything else.

I taught myself to be more feminine--not dainty or meek--
but beautifully bold.
Studied Nina Simone and Maya Angelou.
Held my neck erect
let flashes of limber legs peek through my skirts
trained my deep voice to meander every consonant and vowel
swayed hips west to east in my jaunts around town
and was still single.
I had my teary nights of picking myself and my choices apart but
my heart kept beating
synapses kept firing
neurons commanded--
Move!
and every day I was

arising/eating/bathing/gazing/grooming/confabulating/giving/living/
loving me.

You do know that you're beautiful, right?

We've been reclaiming strength, glory, womanhood
since we were dragged up from the bowels of slave ships onto these stolen shores,
since Sojourner bared her muscles to demonstrate the strength of her arm
exposed her breast to doubters of her womanliness.

160 years later
Bigots called you an ape when Ghostbusters came out.
Before Christian Siriano adorned your curves in red,
most designers refused to dress you for the film's premiere
because you're not a "sample size".

That Allstate commercial has you embodying the Jezebel trope.

Why else did the director have
the white man who pulled up in a car beside you
widen his blue eyes in terror when you offered your phone number,
show you flirt with a tow truck driver
who doesn't respond to your smile,
sassy invitation: You must be Jerry. Heyyyy.

Why didn't you yell "Cut!"? Tell the scriptwriters--
Excuse me, but you all need to keep this real.
What single woman is going to come on to a tow truck driver?
She is going to be too busy texting her sisters,
her best girlfriends to tell them where she is for safety's sake,
trying to get a ride home from the auto shop,
figuring out how to pay for repairs.

And I know you were asking yourself--
why is Lupita beautiful (deeply brown too, but petite) and not me?
You believed it would soothe you to laugh through your pain
for your Saturday Night Live debut:

Back in the slave days, I woulda NEVER been single!

I'm six feet tall and I'm strong, Colin. STRONG!
I mean, look at me. I'm a Mandingo!
Massa woulda hooked me up with the strongest brother on the plantation!
Every nine months I woulda been popping them out: Shaq, Kobe, LeBron.

Among the Mandingo--or the Mandinka--
sons of Sundiata, the Lion King of Mali, and Mansa Musa,
Shaq, Kobe, LeBron would have been average men.
What kind of special would you have been popping out for Massa
that he wouldn't wrench from your arms to sell off or work to death?
They matter here and now to them because they, traded from master to
master, can play basketball.

Colin Jost--your delicious coconut milkshake--
sitting there grinning, audience laughter in the background.
I'm used to white noise drowning out black pain--
But you, a number one slave draft pick?

You, of the runaway tongue--
"I don't want to be a slave.
I don't like working for you white folks right now, and y'all pay me"--
would have been stripped,
your back opened up at the whipping post
salt, brine, or hot wax thrown in your wounds to cure you.

If Massa,
his sons,
his overseers,
his neighbors,
his visitors didn't rape you,
think he would have given you time
to choose, to jump the broom
with a man you loved, loved you back,
who would coax you to satisfaction however, whenever you wanted?

The stud Massa would have chosen for you
might have rushed to get it over with
because he had a wife of his own he loved, wanted to get back to,
knew Massa could have/would have been watching or listening to ensure
strong black bodies for the auction block or the fields.

How could you call it a Love Life?

Did you ever hear the one about the slave mother who
led her seven children to the auction block
to see them all sold away?
She cried, Why don't the Lord kill me now?

You forgot why Margaret Garner
slaughtered her daughter with a butcher knife
and was going to kill the rest of her babies before the slavecatchers stopped
her?

Did making light of our foremothers' heavy swallow up your lonely?

Before I became Baby Girl,
I was feeling like men, especially our men, weren't feeling me.
I was too smart too tough
too strong too independent too stubborn
too absent from the kitchen,
insufficiently pretty or graceful.

I asked an elder what's causing tension between black men and women:
Women should feed a man's ego.
My mother used to sneak in the kitchen, slip lemon juice
into Papa's barbecue sauce that he bragged on.
He used to ask her, "Isn't mine the best?"
She used to say "Yes, yours is the best, honey"
never revealing how she spiced it up.

I thought,
Why must we be like a speck of stellar dust in a man's galaxy?

No such thing as being too large to love, and no sin in loudness.
Don't we blast our favorite songs?

Someday your warrior
that can make you laugh
will find you.

Whet

One day he looked at me and said,
"Explain why men and women
don't get along and what would you do about it."

Since we're still in that sugary sobriquet/
no arguing/hugged up while sleeping/
hand holding/kissing in public phase,

I wondered what the shelf life
on this new happiness would be.

My face must have fallen because then he was saying,
"Come here."
Lead me by my hand to the bed,

laid down on the sheets, pulling me still, saying
"Kneel over me,"

and then he was like
a bee in a honey sac.

I whispered,
why do you love this so much?

"Because you're
mango-coco-cherry sweet,

because even the surface of the Earth
is 70 percent water."

Looking down on him,
under me, hands upstretched,
fingers grasping my thighs,
like he is at worship,

I thought, *this could be the answer.*

For The Lovers

As usual, journalists do what Big Business won't.
Chirography in soil: *I am only 15*.
Since two-thirds of the world's cocoa
is produced by the hands of two million West African children,
and after twenty years the corporations
can't keep the pledge to eradicate child labor,
chocolates should come wrapped in tattered rags.
Those of us who eat it should be compelled to drink water
that looks like milk
out of a dirty bucket.
All chocolate should be white like the cocoa beans it comes from.
It doesn't deserve the beauty of brown.
Chocolates should taste like
      the sour salt of sweat,
      the tears of boys that miss their mothers, fathers, villages, and home-cooked meals,
      the dirt embedded underneath their fingernails and in their second-hand clothes,
      the blood that oozes when they cut themselves.
Hands that should be holding pencils and books
clench knives to cut open cocoa pods,
swing machetes against tall grasses to clear the land.
They fall asleep to the rhythm of back spasms.
For Mars

Nestle
Hershey
Godiva
to make suffering sweet,
in Nicaragua, Costa Rica, Brazil, and Belize,
children join their parents in the fields,
blistered hand in blistered hand,
risking dehydration, heat stress, chronic kidney disease.
How many more will wave,
yell Mwen Byen as they leave Haiti
for 12-hour days in the bayetes of the Dominican Republic.
No electricity,
running water,
indoor toilets.
The bending and rising at the waist,
the swish and clang of machete against cane,
from the wax, to the wane of the sun.
Safe from the loss of lus soli.
Mwen Byen.

Blood and Soil

I.

Blood.
He said Megyn Kelly had it coming out of her eyes,
her wherever,
because he resented her questions during the debates.
If not for menstrual blood,
men would go the way of the sea mink.

As a daughter, him
promising 17-year-old Ivanka he would never date anyone younger than her,
not punching Howard Stern out for calling her a piece of ass at 22,
saying if she weren't his daughter he'd possibly be dating her,
thinking ownership justified barging in on Miss America contestants as they dressed,
bragging about pussy grabbing,

makes me raise my hands in gratitude to God
for granting me my blue-collar father
whose 6' 3" frame shielded me from illicit gaze,
who taught me I descended from tillers of soil, from
Dahia al-Kahina, Amina Sukhera.
He demanded I lead by speaking my mind, wielding my pen.

II.

Soil.
If he/his ilk understood what George Washington Carver knew--
plant one kind of crop, like cotton, soil gets sick from nitrogen loss.
It thrives on variety--sweet potatoes, peanuts, soybeans.

What does that overprivileged son-of-a-Scottish fisherman's daughter
think America would have been
with only wealthy white Anglo-Saxon men/meek white women?

III.

"They don't look like Indians to me, sir!"
A cornucopia of Native American foods feeds us--
potatoes, beans, corn, peanuts, pumpkins, tomatoes,
squash, peppers, nuts, melons, sunflower seeds.
Their farming methods: 60% of the world's food supply.
Division of power between federal and local government?
The Iroquois League of Nations.
Sign language, tobacco, cigars, pipes, snowshoes, bunk beds, kayaks, canoes,
lacrosse, ice hockey, and field hockey.
Anesthetics.
Salicin from American black willow bark for aspirin.
Names: Milwaukee, Mississippi, Miami, Seattle, Spokane.
In exchange, the Wasicu gave them blankets laced with smallpox.
Broke treaties, stole the most fertile land, passed the Indian Removal Act.
Starvation, pneumonia, smallpox, malaria, measles, cholera,
whooping cough
killed thousands on the Trail of Tears.
Fearing the Ghost Dance, the cavalry shot Sitting Bull in the head at
Wounded Knee.
More than 150 Lakota men/women perished in the bloody mud;
some, mothers with babies nestled to their breasts. The death of Black Elk's
dream.
L. Frank Baum (that wonderful *Wizard of Oz*)
called for the" untamed, untamable redskins" to be wiped off the face of the
earth.
"Kill the Indian, Save the Man" boarding schools chopped off their hair, beat
them
for speaking native tongues.
Navajo Code Talkers helped win the Battle of Iwo Jima
during World War II,
COINTELPRO set up members of AIM to be incarcerated.
Nobody's more for the Indians than Donald Trump,
and Leonard Peltier is likely to die in prison.
In cities, on the reservations, they fight on to preserve their languages,
educate their children, honor their elders.
Spurred by prophecy, many tribes united to cut the head
off the Black Snake.

IV.

"What do you have to lose by trying something new, like Trump?

What would American banks, textile, shipping, insurance, its palette be
without the rice, cotton, tobacco, sugar
planted and harvested by Africa's ebon sons and daughters?
How many blue bloods in graves without milk wrested from African teats?
Denied 400,000 acres and mules,
given under-resourced schools.
Sharecropping for the landless, chain gangs,
poll tax, literacy tests as barriers to poll boxes,
Black people kept giving America gifts.
The blues.
Rotary blades for the lawn mower, carbon filament for the light bulb,
shoe lasting machine, mop, automatic elevator doors,
lawn sprinkler design, ice box for the refrigerator, mobile refrigeration, gas
heating furnace.
Black minds and hands rendered the railway crossing guard signal,
the metal bar that halts vehicles at train tracks, the railway switching device,
but
Black people still had to sit in the back of railway cars with their luggage
around their feet.
We gave America the mailbox, gas mask, and 350,000 of us served in World
War I.
In return, America celebrated *Birth of a Nation*.
Turned its back on the burning crosses.
Black bodies hung like ornaments from oak/pine trees by the thousands,
white mobs hungry to cut themselves a trophy of an ear, finger, phallus,
pose for pictures, or set the bodies aflame,
like Mary Turner,
because she threatened to have the men who lynched her innocent husband
arrested.
To teach her/millions of her sisters a lesson, the mob hung her upside down,
sliced her pregnant belly open, let the fetus fall, stomped it to death with
their boots,
shot hundreds of bullets into her 19-year-old body.
The mickle of spilled black blood the next year: James Weldon Johnson
called it the Red Summer.
Jazz and the Charleston got America swinging, swigging cocktails;

white mobs murdered, looted, burned black prosperity from Greenwood to
Rosewood.
And black people kept on giving:
traffic light, rock and roll, foil electric microphone, blood banks and
bloodmobiles.

If laid side by side, HeLa cells could wrap around the circumference of the
earth in a three-tiered hug.
A cure for polio, treatments for tuberculosis and influenza, Parkinson's
disease, HIV,
an HPV vaccine that could have saved Henrietta's life, and her family lives in
poverty.

Successful open-heart surgery, the pacemaker, lasers for cataract removal,
automatic gear shift for cars, home security system, touch tone phone, caller
ID, call waiting
gamma electrical cell for cellular phones, synthesis of physostigmine to treat
glaucoma
synthesis of progesterone and testosterone from plant sterols for birth
control pills and corticosteroids,
video game consoles.
Black America's CNN co-opted as commercial soundtrack:
liquor, sneakers, clothes, insurance, cars.
Gave America its greatest modern president, but
George Zimmerman walks free,
Mumia sure to die behind bars,
and most white voters/the electoral college chose a man who sums us up
thusly:
*You're living in poverty, your schools are no good, you have no jobs, 58% of your youth
is unemployed. What the hell do you have to lose?"*

V.

*"When Mexico sends its people, it doesn't send its very best...They're bringing drugs,
they're bringing crime, they're rapists. And some, I assume are good people."*

Latinos have been in America since the beginning:
Thousands of Spanish soldiers bled and died during
the Revolutionary War.

Bernardo de Galvez, his army of Spanish and Cuban soldiers, Choctaw Indians, and black former slaves beat off the British attack in 1780 and gained control of the Mississippi River.
Cubans helped fund America's victory at the Battle of Yorktown.
As the sons and daughters of Puerto Rico, the Dominican Republic, Ecuador, El Salvador
came North fleeing poverty, political repression, violence erupting from American-backed coups,
they were segregated in slums, schools,
subject to the policeman's nightstick.
Brought in as braceros to fill the void of farm laborers,
millions deported back to Mexico with policies like Operation Wetback.
No Latinos, and no
cowboys or cattle ranching,
dollar symbol,
State of Texas,
Southern-style barbecue,
color TV,
Mendez v. Westminster to help desegregate California schools (before Brown vs. Board of Ed),
country-western music without the Mexican rancheras,
ballroom dancing without mambo, rumba, tango, merengue,
and cha-cha-cha,
successful exploration of Mars,
modern-day theory of mass extinction of the dinosaurs,
synthesis of RNA,
understanding of chlorofluorocarbons.

VI.

Donald J. Trump is calling for a total and complete shutdown of Muslims entering the United States until our country's representatives find out what the hell is going on. We have no choice.

The father of modern surgery? A 10th-Century Muslim physician from Spain.
Muslims fought for George Washington in the Revolutionary War.
American marching bands originated in the Ottoman Empire.
The violin evolved from Islamic bowing instruments.

Without them, no
ice cream cones
tubular structures for American skyscrapers like the Sears Tower,
intraventricular catheter system for the aspiration of cerebrospinal fluid for
the delivery of drugs
Ommaya Reservoir to provide chemotherapy to the site of brain tumors,
coma score for classification of traumatic brain injury,
National Center for Injury Prevention and Control,
and one-tenth of the doctors in America would disappear.

VII.

"Every vagina is a landmine. Haven't we both said that in private?"
-Howard Stern to a laughing Donald Trump

Since America's inception, men have misunderstood/misconstrued
we women.
Spent millions to land on the moon, and still dismissing
the magic of its magnetic sway over matters of the mind/menstrual blood,
the way we birth both ideas or/and babies.
Unless one of the thousands of mentally ill, poor, and of color
sterilized by deceit or by force--
at home with midwives by candle/kerosene lamp
or with doctors under fluorescent hospital lights--
women peopled this nation,
taught its children,
ministered sick relatives and neighbors in homes and hospitals.
Soil. Fingered it, plant roots, ensuring fertility/fecundity to feed themselves,
families.
Denied rights to property and personhood, many raised their voices in
thunderous waves,
secreted slaves to freedom, marched for the right to vote.
Hunched over sewing machines in factories like Blanck and Harris' Triangle
Shirtwaist.
Paid their fellow immigrants $15 per week for 12-hour daily shifts, refused
to install sprinklers.
The rotted fire hose with rusty valve yielded no water
to extinguish the fire.

145 mostly female workers fell down the elevator shaft,
burned to death in the stairwell behind its locked (thief-proof) door,
jumped in groups of two or three to their deaths on the sidewalk when the
life nets ripped.
Moved by photographs of broken bodies entangled in skirts,
New York, other cities passed better safety and fire codes, but the men of the
grand jury
refused to honor their unintended sacrifice by indicting the owners.
And still women had to challenge the notion that men had bigger, therefore
better, brains.
Helen Gardener bequeathed hers to Cornell, proving women as intelligent
as men,
and the Equal Rights Amendment dies every year.
Half a century has not passed since women had options
beyond secret knocks on back doors,
bitter teas, bleach, turpentine, acid, motor oil,
knitting needles, pens, coat hangers, bicycle spokes.
Without women, there would be no
Battle Hymn of the Republic
modern nursing
Red Cross
Apgar score
frequency hopping
discovery of the dangers of DDT
purinethol to treat leukemia
discovery of the double helix in DNA
genetic transposition or charting of the frontal lobe of the brain.

VIII.

"Thank you for your interest in the subject.
-The White House LGBTQ page

LGBTQ people,
ostracized, arrested, beaten, murdered for who and how they love.
Without them,
None of Baron von Steuben's military tactics to help win the Revolutionary
War.
No "America the Beautiful" or Symphony No. 3,

"In Cold Blood",
"Breakfast at Tiffany's",
"The Glass Menagerie" and "A Streetcar Named Desire",
"I Too, Sing America",
"West Side Story",
15 minutes of fame,
"Hairspray".
Modern computer science
Nonviolent tactics in the Civil Rights Movement and the March on Washington.
Nonoxynol-9 as spermicide.

IX.

What if Scottish immigrants were called rapists
run off American soil
a trans-Atlantic barrier built between America and Scotland
so Trump's mother couldn't come here as a maid,
meet a man who made a fortune in real estate
(locked black people out),
and then have a maid of her own?

X.

Despite
ending the Obama-era equal pay rule,
attempts to defund/destroy Planned Parenthood,
the Global Gag Rule depriving aid to organizations that inform women about abortions,
attempts to repeal the Affordable Care Act,
arguing in federal court that gay rights in the workplace are not covered by Title VII,
the transgender ban in the military,
appointing Betsy DeVos to the Department of Education and aiming to cut $9 billion from its budget,
denying climate change,
pulling out of the Paris Climate Agreement,

trying to greenlight the Dakota Access and Keystone pipelines,
eliminating the Obama-era federal flood risk management standard,
appointing bigots as Attorney General and Chief Strategist,
trying to build that border wall Mexico will never pay for,
the refugee ban,
undermining affirmative action,
dismantling of DACA,
calling the destruction of Confederate symbols foolish,
calling the all-white/alt-right that protest their destruction "very fine people",
the vehicular murder of Heather Heyer,
the beating of Deandre Green,
not apologizing to the Central Park Five for demanding they get the death penalty,
the return of selling military equipment to the police,
the murders of Deborah Braillard and Felix Torres
and pardon of Sheriff Arpaio,
American people of color
women
non-binary people are living/loving/procreating/innovating/teaching/building/legislating/
organizing.

Cities are swapping Columbus Day for Indigenous People's Day.
Statues in his likeness, strewn with artificial blood
in Buffalo, Houston, Manhattan,
busted with sledgehammers in Baltimore and Yonkers,
shards of symbol littering soil.

Love, by the numbers

One hundred years after suffrage, more than half of white women voted for Trump,
longing for the days when 200 women a year drank poison, threw themselves down stairs, and died,
damn the word-of-mouth to midwives and doctors that surreptitiously ended 20-25% of pregnancies.
They and their husbands pine for lying tongues, pointing fingers, economic jealousy to burn black towns, set nooses around Black bodies, slice-open bellies, stomp out fetuses, body parts in a jar as heirloom.
Bring back stop-and-frisk and chokeholds for safe streets! Swing batons like battering rams!

There is a fluttering in my chest.

Ruth held on as long as she could, but six conservatives sit on the Supreme Court.
Separated at the border, five hundred parents still cry and pray every night for reunion with their children.
Republicans and Democrats supervised the election, and Republicans like Graham cry fraud.
For now, no one needs to sit in bed like my father, propped against pillow, health insurance revoked, on the phone with his insurance company. "But I have cancer." Multiple myeloma.
Seventy-seven million spoke, and all eyes are on Ossoff and Warnock in Georgia.
Two hundred fifty thousand dead from COVID-19, and counting.
Unemployment and evictions on the rise.

There is a fluttering in my chest.

But on November 7, 2020, as pots clanged, horns honked from
Oakland to Chicago to Philly to Times Square:
red, white, and blue flags, red, black, and green flags,
rainbow flags unfurled side by side.
Drumming/singing/clapping/dancing the cha cha slide,
Black/brown/white skin-on-skin, gender-to-gender.
Joe jogged forward. Kamala waved.
Something that felt like love swayed beneath my rib cage.

There is a fluttering in my chest.

Scattered Legacy

Toni Morrison owned books just like me. Among the 1,200, no cracked spines. No dog-eared pages. Notes where I needed 'em. I understand selling her apartment, but if she had been my mother, I would spend the rest of my life cracking them open. Smell the paper, praying for a hint of her perfume. Reading the titles I hadn't already read and re-reading my favorites.

The

BluestEye.Sula.SongofSolomon.TarBaby.Jazz.Beloved.Paradise.Love. The BluestEye.Sula.SongofSolomon.TarBaby.Jazz.Beloved.Paradise. Love.The BluestEye.Sula.SongofSolomon.TarBaby.Jazz.Beloved.Paradise.Love.The BluestEye.Sula.SongofSolomon.TarBaby.Jazz.Beloved.Paradise.Love.

When Uncle Reggie died, I stacked his hardcover classics of the canon, from Faust to Twain, on the bottom shelf of the bookcase with Daddy's books, which take up the top five shelves. When Daddy died, Donna and I divided his books. She kept his novels. I took health, homeopathy, cancer care, Cone and Felder, Van Sertima and Ben-Jochanan.

The

BluestEye.Sula.SongofSolomon.TarBaby.Jazz.Beloved.Paradise.Love. The BluestEye.Sula.SongofSolomon.TarBaby.Jazz.Beloved.Paradise. Love.The BluestEye.Sula.SongofSolomon.TarBaby.Jazz.Beloved.Paradise.Love.The BluestEye.Sula.SongofSolomon.TarBaby.Jazz.Beloved.Paradise.Love.

When Donna died, I went up and down the floor-to-ceiling shelves in her office at Macmillan. Took all the books I could find with her name on the acknowledgments page. Her favorite pens, notepads with her publication notes, and her favorite mugs. One box of turmeric tea and one box of jasmine. Like me, she couldn't stand straight coffee. Tea was my bag!

The

BluestEye.Sula.SongofSolomon.TarBaby.Jazz.Beloved.Paradise.Love. The BluestEye.Sula.SongofSolomon.TarBaby.Jazz.Beloved.Paradise. Love.The BluestEye.Sula.SongofSolomon.TarBaby.Jazz.Beloved.Paradise.Love.The BluestEye.Sula.SongofSolomon.TarBaby.Jazz.Beloved. Paradise.Love.

The thought of Toni's scattered legacy makes me want to take pictures of my six bookshelves and several hundred titles. Send the photos to my best friend, tell her, even if I get rich or famous as a poet:

Don't you let them sell my books when I'm gone.

Afterword

Honeysuckle Me happened when I fell in love in the spring of 2017, and it flowed like water into almost every poem I was writing. This collection was intended to be a chapbook of short poems celebrating romance and sensuality.

Once the seeds of other poems were planted and emerged as new work, I welcomed them here because I saw love in this work about the spices in my kitchen, my mother, teaching, dancing, and my hair. I wanted to reach out to comedian Leslie Jones through my poem "Sister to Sister" after what I found to be a problematic sketch on *Saturday Night Live*. I was deeply enraged by the sexism and racism of the 45th presidential administration, but I channeled my angst into my epic poem "Blood and Soil" to memorialize the contributions that people of color, women, and queer people have made to the United States since its inception.

I hope you enjoyed this book. Thank you for your support.

The Author

Carla M. Cherry is a native of the Bronx, NY. A graduate of Spelman College, New York University, and Lehman College, she has been teaching in the New York City public schools since 1996. Her poetry has appeared in various publications, including Anderbo, Eunoia Review, Dissident Voice, Random Sample Review, Firefly Magazine, Picaroon Poetry, Streetlight Press, MemoryHouse, Bop Dead City, Ariel Chart, Anti-Heroin Chic, The Racket, and Raising Mothers. All five of her books of poetry were published by ii-Publishing, which includes: *Gnat Feathers and Butterfly Wings, Thirty Dollars and a Bowl of Soup, Honeysuckle Me, These Pearls Are Real*, and *Stardust and Skin*. She is an M.F.A. candidate in Creative Writing at the City College of New York.

CONNECT WITH ME:

Email: carla.cherrybxpoet@gmail.com
Website: www.carlacherrybxpoet1.com
Facebook: @poeticchic
Twitter: @carla_bronxpoet
Instagram: @carlabxpoet1

Publication Credits

"Explorers" and "Guilt" originally appeared in Street Light Press.

"Pyrophobia" originally appeared in Issue #11 of Picaroon Poetry in November 2017.

"A Little Magic" originally appeared in Issue #11 of Firefly magazine.

"Flourish" originally appeared in 433 magazine.

"Diastema" originally appeared in Terra Preta Review.

"Tattoo" and "Pith" originally appeared in Writer's Egg magazine.

"For the Lovers" originally appeared in Down in the Dirt magazine and the Blogging Carnival for Nonviolence in 2019.

"Bobbing" will appear in Sledgehammer Literary Journal.

www.ingramcontent.com/pod-product-compliance
Lightning Source LLC
Chambersburg PA
CBHW062140100526
44589CB00014B/1633